Does It Really Rain Frogs?

Thomas Canavan

ARCTURUS

This edition first published in 2014 by Arcturus Publishing
Reprinted in 2015

Distibuted by Black Rabbit Books
P.O. Box 3263
Mankato
Minnesota MN 56002

Printed in the United States

Library of Congress Cataloging-in-Publication Data

Canavan, Thomas.
 Does it really rain frogs? : questions and answers about planet Earth / Thomas Canavan.
     p. cm. -- (Science FAQ)
 Audience: Grade 4 to 6.
 Summary: "Answers common questions young readers have about weather, space, and other
phenomena of planet Earth"-- Provided by publisher.
 Includes index.
 ISBN 978-1-78212-393-4 (library binding)
 1. Earth sciences--Juvenile literature. 2. Children's questions and answers. 3. Earth--Miscellanea--
Juvenile literature. I. Title.
 QE29.C354 2014
 550.2--dc23
                            2013004703

Editor: Joe Harris
Picture researcher: Joe Harris
Designer: Ian Winton

Picture credits: All images supplied by Shutterstock.

SL002660US
Supplier 02, Date 1014, Print Run 3838

Contents

Home sweet globe

Do you have a globe in your bedroom or classroom? Take a good look at it. Can you imagine being an astronaut, watching the real Earth floating in space? It's an amazing thought, isn't it!

Why does it get hotter in the summer?

During spring and summer, the northern hemisphere (the Earth's top half) is tilted toward the Sun. It gets more sunlight and becomes hotter. At this time, the southern hemisphere has the fall and winter. Then things swap six months later when the bottom half is closer to the Sun.

Why is most of the world's land north of the equator?

It just happens to be that way at the moment. Believe it or not, the Earth's continents are slowly moving. Around 300 million years ago, our planet had one big mass of land called Pangaea. It was mainly south of the equator. In another 200 million years, things will probably look different again.

How much of the Earth is covered by ice?

Just under 10 percent. Most of that ice is in the glaciers and ice caps of Greenland and Antarctica. Snow and ice also cover mountains in other parts of the world all year long.

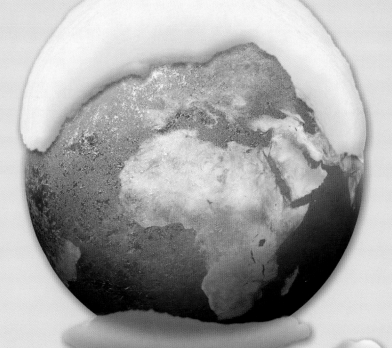

How far away is the horizon?

It depends on your height! The taller, or higher up, you are, the farther you'll be able to see before the curve of the Earth dips out of sight. For a girl who is 4 foot 7 inches (1.4 m) tall, the horizon would be 2.6 miles (4.2 km) away. But if she stood on a 10 foot (3 m) ladder, the horizon would be 4.6 miles (7.5 km) away.

5

Stormy weather

Help! Frogs are bouncing off my umbrella! Straws are flying by like spears, and my ears are ringing from all that thunder! And I thought the weather forecast said "a slight chance of a shower."

Does it really rain frogs?

Yes, but not very often. A very powerful storm can suck frogs and fish up from rivers, lakes, and the sea. They are held up by strong, spinning winds. Then they fall back down when the winds weaken.

Can the wind really drive a straw through a telegraph pole?

Yes, it can, if the wind is strong enough. And tornado winds blow at more than 300 miles per hour (500 km/h). Harmless objects can then become deadly weapons. But isn't a straw too weak? Not if one end is blocked. Then the air rushes in and pushes out on the sides. The straw gets stronger, just like a pumped-up bike tire.

Is the saying "Red sky at night, sailors' delight" really accurate?

Yes, it often is. Rain clouds usually travel from west to east. They look red when the Sun is low. A "red sky at night" means that the Sun's rays are shining on clouds that have already passed to the east. This means that it is less likely to be stormy the next day.

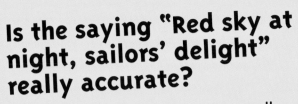

Does every thunderstorm have lightning?

The answer is very simple—yes. Lightning causes thunder. A lightning bolt quickly heats up air. The hot air expands and then quickly cools and contracts. That superfast heating and cooling makes the sound of thunder.

Around and around

Our home, the Earth, is whizzing through
space, spinning around twice as fast as a plane.
Does that make you feel dizzy?
You might want to shout,
"Stop the world,
I want to get off!"

Why don't people in the southern hemisphere fall off?

People in the southern hemisphere are not upside down. It's just that most maps are drawn with the southern hemisphere at the bottom. An upside-down map would be just as accurate. In fact, gravity pulls everything toward the center of the Earth, so we all stay on it!

Why don't we feel the Earth spinning?

The Earth rotates (spins) completely around once every 24 hours. That means that it's spinning at 1,070 miles per hour (1,670 km/h). However, we don't feel that motion because we're also moving at the same speed. It's like traveling in a plane—you don't feel like you're moving fast.

Is the Earth slowing down?

Yes, it is. The exact length of a day (one complete spin of the planet) on Earth is 23 hours and 56 minutes. However, the Earth is slowing down by about one second every ten years. So in 2,400 years, a day really will last exactly 24 hours.

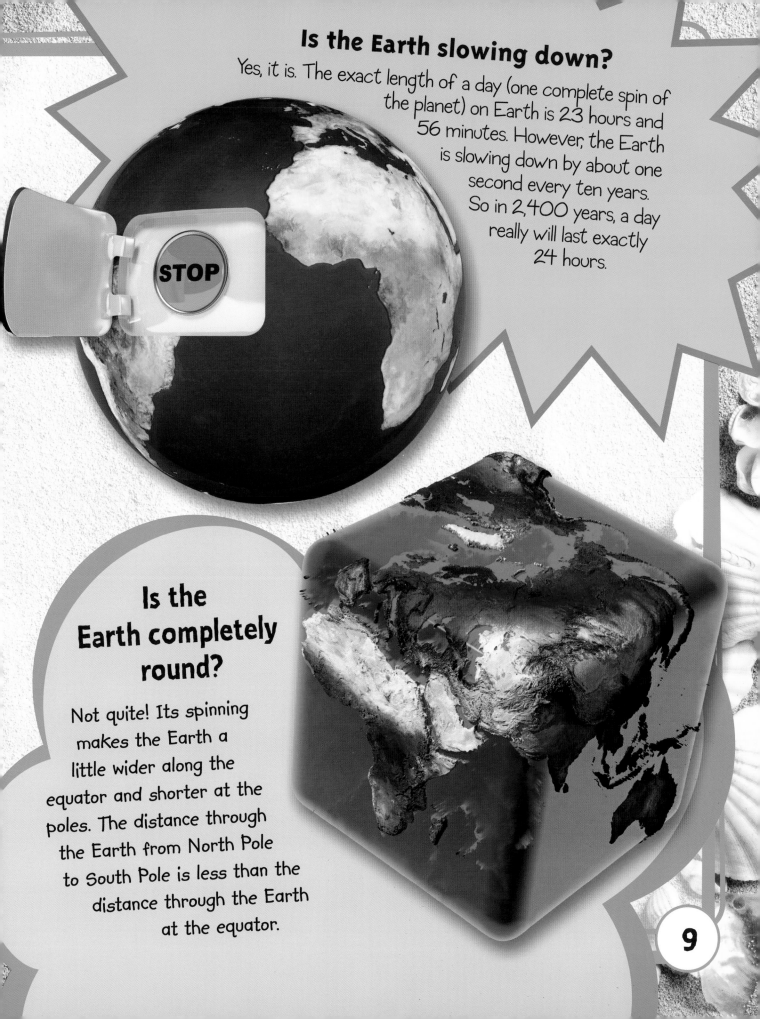

Is the Earth completely round?

Not quite! Its spinning makes the Earth a little wider along the equator and shorter at the poles. The distance through the Earth from North Pole to South Pole is less than the distance through the Earth at the equator.

The right impression

We can definitely trust our eyes and ears, can't we, when it comes to the world around us? Well, not always! It's time for us to investigate weird happenings such as echoes and mirages.

What is an echo?

An echo is simply a reflection of sound just as a mirror image is a reflection of light. Sound travels in waves. When these waves hit a hard surface, they bounce back. We hear the sound again a little later (once it has traveled to the hard surface and back).

Why does the Moon seem so big when it's just rising over the horizon?

Scientists know that it's a trick that our eyes play on us. However, they can't agree on how it works. To show that the Moon doesn't change size, hold a coin out so it just covers the Moon on the horizon. Hold it at the same distance when the Moon is overhead. You won't see any change in size.

Why do we see mirages in the desert?

A mirage is an image that we see because light rays have been refracted (bent). In the desert, light from the Sun sometimes bounces up from a layer of hot, low air. What we see is really an image of the sky, but to us it looks like water on the ground.

Do you really hear the ocean if you put a seashell to your ear?

What you hear are the sounds around you—background noise. These sounds are bouncing around inside the shell. You hear those bounced-around sounds as a "whoosh," and your brain decides it's the sound of the ocean. Why? Probably because you're holding a seashell.

A large shake, please

The Earth beneath your feet may seem solid and steady. However, our planet's surface is in constant movement. Sometimes that movement results in earthquakes and volcanoes.

Can animals predict earthquakes?

The answer seems to be "yes" for some animals. Frogs and toads can sense slight chemical changes in the water in ponds or lakes. Scientists have noticed similar changes in rocks in the days leading up to earthquakes. Witnesses have seen groups of toads leaving ponds just before earthquakes.

Why do volcanoes **erupt?**

The Earth's crust (outer layer) is made up of large pieces called plates. Magma, a gooey substance made up of gas and melted rock, lies under the plates. When two plates collide, they may force magma to the surface in a volcanic eruption. The magma that comes out is called lava.

Why do South America and Africa look like pieces of a jigsaw puzzle?

All of the continents were once part of one large landmass. However, the Earth's crust is constantly moving. This movement broke up the giant landmass millions of years ago. The edges of some continents show us where the continents were once joined.

Africa

South America

Could flowing lava really overtake a car?

The speed of a lava flow differs from volcano to volcano. A lot depends on how steep the slope is. The amount of gas mixed in with the molten (melted) rock also affects how "runny" the lava is. Witnesses have recorded lava flowing faster than 38 miles per hour (60 km/h)—fast enough to overtake a car.

Forcing the issue

Everything on Earth is affected by forces. Whether it's the force of gravity that makes things fall, the magnetic force that guides metal, or the electrical forces that produce lightning, they put on quite a show.

Do planes get struck by lightning?

Passenger planes get hit by lightning about once a year. Luckily, the lightning usually has no bad effect on the plane or passengers. It just leaves a scorch mark where it first hits. The electrical charge travels along the outside of the plane. Most lightning strikes occur when planes are below 3 miles (5 km). Planes usually avoid trouble by flying higher than this.

Would a penny dropped from a skyscraper make a hole in the sidewalk below?

All objects accelerate (travel faster and faster) as they fall. If nothing slowed it down, a penny would be traveling at about 200 miles per hour (320 km/h) after falling from one of the tallest skyscrapers. But its flat shape slows the acceleration. At ground level, the penny is only traveling at about 25 miles per hour (40 km/h). That's too slow to damage the sidewalk.

What are shooting stars?

Shooting stars aren't really stars at all. They're meteors—pieces of rock or ice that have been speeding through space. Gravity draws them toward Earth if they get close. The energy from their movement turns into heat energy. All that heat makes them they glow brightly as they zoom across the sky.

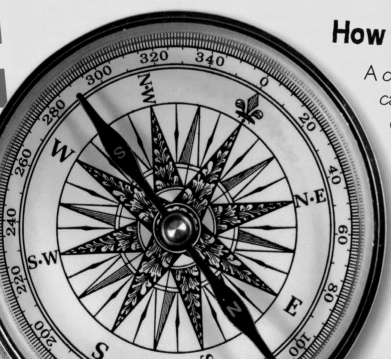

How do compasses work?

A compass is a magnetic needle that can spin freely. It is attracted by other magnets. The compass works because the Earth itself is like a huge magnet. It has magnetic north and south poles. The painted end of the needle always points north.

Just give me some time

We are used to thinking about time in hours and days, but when it comes to Earth science, things happen much more slooooowly. Much of what we see around us has changed over a long time ... and is still changing.

Why are beaches sandy?

Sand is simply rock that has been broken into very small pieces. These pieces are less than 0.08 inch (2 mm) across. Every beach was once made of solid rock. The sea's pounding waves grind coastal rocks into small pieces over thousands of years.

Can plants turn to stone?

The word *petrified* means "turned to stone." This can happen to plants or animals after they have died. Water that has minerals in it dissolves the plant's soft tissue. The harder parts, such as the tubes and bark, don't dissolve. The minerals take less than 100 years to harden. By then, the plant still looks like a plant, but it is now made of stone.

How fast does a glacier move?

Scientists often describe glaciers as being "rivers of ice." Like normal rivers, glaciers flow at different speeds. It depends on the slope of the land, the air temperature, the soil beneath, and many other factors. The fastest, Greenland's Quarayaq glacier, travels up to 80 feet (24 m) a day.

Did a meteorite really kill off the dinosaurs?

Dinosaurs were common across the world for many millions of years. Then all signs of them stopped about 65 million years ago. Their disappearance was a mystery for many years. Most scientists now agree that a large meteorite (a stone from space that crashes to Earth) hit our planet about 65 million years ago. It caused a huge tsunami and sent poisonous gases into the air that killed the dinosaurs.

Lighten up

Without the Sun, our world would be a dark and cold place! The Sun gives off energy in the form of light and heat. Some forms of light energy are invisible to us—but they can still affect us!

Why is **snow** white?

Light is made up of different colors. Some colors are absorbed when light hits an object. Other colors are reflected, and those are the colors that we see. When light hits ice crystals, it bounces off, and all the colors are reflected at once. When all the colors are mixed, we see the color white.

Why is the sky blue?

Most of light's colors pass through the sky directly. But gases in the sky absorb blue light and then send it out again. They bounce that blue light in all directions. It's everywhere in the sky, which means that we see a blue sky.

How are we protected from the Sun's rays?

Some of the Sun's radiation is bad for us. Ultraviolet light, for example, harms living things. It causes sunburn and even cancer. Luckily, a layer of the Earth's atmosphere absorbs about 98 percent of this light. This is the ozone layer. The ozone layer is about 12–25 miles (20–40 km) above the Earth's surface.

What causes a rainbow?

After it rains, lots of tiny drops of water still float around in the sky. With the clouds gone, sunlight can shine through again. This light refracts (bends) as it enters each drop. This bending splits up all the different colors. Then these separated colors bounce back out of the drop. So, you see the light after it has been separated by the water drops.

Making a splash

The Earth looks blue when it's viewed from the Moon. That's because two-thirds of its surface is covered with water. Don't be shy—just dive in to find out more about this familiar liquid.

Why do oceans have salt water but rivers have fresh water?

The water in rivers comes from rain. Rainwater does not have any salt in it. The river picks up small amounts of salt from the ground as it travels downhill. This salt enters the ocean at the river mouth. The saltwater mixture becomes saltier as water evaporates.

Are tidal waves and tsunamis the same thing?

No, although many people confuse these two terms. The key is the word *tidal*. Tidal waves are just that—big waves that build up at high tide. A tsunami is a giant wave—or series of waves—caused by an underwater earthquake or volcanic eruption.

TSUNAMI HAZARD ZONE

IN CASE OF EARTHQUAKE GO TO HIGH GROUND OR INLAND

How much does it rain during a monsoon?

An awful lot! A monsoon is a long rainy period. It happens in places where the wind direction changes at the same time each year. India's monsoon develops in late May when the wind shifts to the south. Some areas get more than 2.5 inches (65 mm) of rain in twelve hours.

What causes ocean waves?

Wind passing over water creates waves. The water absorbs some of the wind's energy. However, the ocean's enormous water pressure pushes back up. These two opposite pushes create a wave movement that travels across the ocean.

Rain, rain, go away

Everyone likes to talk about the weather—and to moan about it! So, how would you like to be the one who can provide some answers when others ask, "Do you think it's going to rain this weekend—or this century?"

Are rain forests always in hot places?

The most famous rain forests are in the hot tropical regions of South America, Africa, and Asia. But rain forests also develop in cooler parts of the world, as long as those places get enough rain. The Pacific coast of Canada has the largest temperate rain forest.

Where on Earth is the easiest place to forecast the weather?

The British are always talking about the weather—because it's constantly changing. Other parts of the world, though, have much more constant climates. Probably the easiest place to forecast weather is the Atacama Desert in Chile, where no rain fell between 1571 and 1970.

Can a butterfly's flapping wing really cause a hurricane?

Maybe! The "butterfly effect" describes how a small change, such as the air movement caused by a butterfly's beating wing, can trigger much bigger changes. It works like a series of dominoes, where the first domino is tiny, and the last one is huge. This effect can make the weather very hard to predict.

Why are there more thunderstorms in the summer?

Thunderstorms need two things to form—moisture and rapidly rising warm air. The late spring and summer are the most common times when these conditions occur. That's because those are the times when the Sun is at its hottest. It warms the air more than at any other time of the year.

Now you've done it

The rest of the planet's animals and plants must sometimes think, "It was OK until you humans came along!" It's true that we have had a huge effect on Earth in the short time we've been here.

Can a polluted lake or river become clean again?

Yes, it can. The first step is to make sure that poisonous chemicals, sewage, and other materials can't flow into the lake. Fresh water needs to flow through to keep it clean. Experts can filter the water to get rid of solids. They can also add tiny organisms to restore the balance of gases dissolved in the water.

When will we run out of oil?

Nobody knows for sure. It is hard to say exactly how much oil is left or exactly how fast the world will use what it does find. Many experts believe that very little oil will be left after 2060. The world will need to find alternative sources of energy before then.

Could a nuclear explosion change the Earth's rotation (spinning)?

Nuclear explosions release more energy than anything else that humans do. Luckily, the energy released by a nuclear explosion is only about one-trillionth of the energy of the Earth's spinning. Scientists compare it to trying to slow the speed of a truck by crashing it into a mosquito.

Do coral reefs only form in tropical waters?

Most coral reefs form in shallow tropical waters. However, scientists are now studying mysterious deep coral reefs, which can form in much colder waters. Coral reefs are under threat from pollution and fishing, so many people are working hard to protect them.

25

Going to extremes

Lots of people get their thrills from taking things to the limit. How would you like to experience what life is like at the extremes of our own planet? Make sure you pack some blankets and fans.

What's at the very center of the Earth?

The center of the Earth is a ball of metal (nickel and iron). This is the inner core. It's the last layer that you would find if you peeled away the Earth's crust (the top layer), its mantle (sticky melted rock), and its outer core (liquid rock). The inner core is as hot as the Sun's surface— 10,000°F (5,430°C).

How far from the poles can icebergs go before they melt?

Most icebergs remain in the cold Arctic and Antarctic waters. But currents can take them into warmer areas. Icebergs are common off the Atlantic coast of Canada, and some Arctic icebergs drift as far south as Japan.

Why doesn't the half of the Earth facing away from the Sun freeze every night?

We can thank our atmosphere for keeping us warm. The atmosphere stops most of the Sun's heat from radiating (escaping outward). It acts just like a blanket or comforter to keep us warm. The atmosphere also stops the Earth from getting too hot during the day.

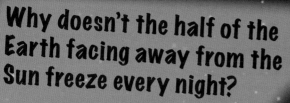

Was the biggest explosion in Earth's history natural or man-made?

The largest man-made explosion was a Russian nuclear weapon exploded in 1961. However, the meteorite that crashed to Earth 65 million years ago and wiped out the dinosaurs made a bigger explosion. It was 1.7 million times more powerful than the Russian weapon.

Air we go

Are these facts about the wind, clouds, and air pressure a load of hot air? Of course not! They're all completely true … and they might just blow you away.

Why don't clouds fall down to Earth?

Clouds are made of millions of tiny drops of water and particles of ice. They are so small that they float in the air. Gravity can't pull them to the ground. But these small bits of ice and water can collide and form larger particles or drops. When they do, they fall to the ground as snow or rain.

Ouch, my ears!

Why do our ears pop in an airplane?

Inside our ears are tiny passages that are filled with air. Normally, this air has the same pressure (outward push) as the air all around us. As we go up in a plane, the air pressure around us gets weaker. But the air inside our ear passages is still the same. The ear has to let air out to change the pressure, and that's what makes our ears pop.

How high up does the atmosphere go?

The atmosphere has five layers. The lowest layer, the troposphere, is where the weather changes. Above it is the stratosphere, where planes travel. Then there's the mesosphere, Earth's shield against meteors. The hot thermosphere is farther out, giving way to the thin exosphere. That outer layer finishes about 6,000 miles (10,000 km) above us.

What makes the wind blow?

Some parts of the atmosphere are warmer than others. Cold air has a higher pressure than warm air (this means it pushes outward harder). So cold air always tries to force its way into areas of warmer air. The wind we feel is air doing just that. If there's a big difference in air pressure, then the wind will be strong.

Glossary

absorb to soak up or suck up

atmosphere the layers of gases that surround the Earth, providing protection and helping to control the planet's temperature

contract to draw together by shrinking or making tighter

dissolve to mix together completely with a liquid and form a solution

equator the imaginary line around the Earth, halfway between the North Pole and the South Pole

forecast to predict something, such as the weather

glacier a mass of ice formed by years of falling snow, moving slowly downward like a river of ice

gravity the force that draws objects toward each other

hemisphere Either of the two imaginary halves of the Earth, usually describing one of the halves either north or south of the equator

horizon the line that marks the visible boundary between the Earth and the sky

iceberg a large, floating chunk of ice that has broken off a glacier or mass of ice

ice cap a thick sheet of ice that forms over a wide area

lava rock that has been heated until it melts, then flows through cracks in the Earth's crust when a volcano erupts

magnetic describing a force like an electrical force, which causes certain objects to be attracted to each other

mineral a substance that is made in the earth that is not an animal or plant

plate one of the large pieces of the Earth's crust; the plates move slowly across the planet's surface and cause earthquakes when they collide

radiation the process of sending off waves of energy

reflection the image or sound of something that has bounced back off another surface

scorch to change the color of something by burning it

solution a mixture of one solid, liquid, or gas inside another one

temperate describing a region or climate that is neither too hot nor too cold

tornado very strong winds that form a funnel shape

tropical describing the warm regions of the Earth near the equator

tsunami a huge wave that is caused by a volcano or earthquake under the sea

Further Reading

Basher Science: Planet Earth: What Planet Are You On? by Simon Basher and Dan Gilpin (Kingfisher Publishing, 2010)

Climate Change: Shifting Glaciers, Deserts, and Climate Belts by Timothy Kusky (Facts on File, 2008)

Howling Hurricanes (Awesome Forces of Nature) by Louise Spilsbury and Richard Spilsbury (Heinemann-Raintree, 2010)

National Geographic Kids Everything Weather: Facts, Photos, and Fun that Will Blow You Away by Kathy Furgang (National Geographic Children's Books, 2012)

Web Sites

Earthforce
www.fi.edu/earth/earth.html
The world-renowned Franklin Institute has compiled a powerhouse web site to cover all areas of earthquakes, volcanoes, and plate tectonics. Up-to-the-minute monitoring helps pinpoint volcanic hot spots as they become active.

Exploratorium
www.exploratorium.edu/explore
The excellent Explore section of San Francisco's fun and informative Emploratorium web site takes you through an attention-grabbing collection of webcasts, games, illustrations, and experiments, leading to effortless learning about Earth science, space science, and more.

National Weather Service Weather Forecast Office: Weather for Kids
www.crh.noaa.gov/ gid/?n=weatherforkids
Learn all about lightning, tornadoes, floods, and winter storms, with activities, information, and more.

Windows to the Universe
www.windows2universe.org
A site managed by the U.S. National Earth Science Teachers Association subdivides into many specialist areas, all clearly presented with an eye to holding young people's interest.

Index